Bud's Easy™

Note Taking System

HOW TO TAKE GREAT NOTES IN CLASS
AND
FROM TEXTBOOKS

And

Become an A+ Student

Bud's Easy™

Note Taking System

HOW TO TAKE GREAT NOTES IN CLASS AND FROM TEXTBOOKS

And

Become an A+ Student

Fourth Edition

James Roberts

Lawrence House Publishers
Larchmont, New York 10538

How to Take Great Notes in Class and From Textbooks

Fourth Edition

ISBN 978-1-891707-09-4

Published by Lawrence House Publishers
Larchmont, New York 10538

Contents

Chapter 3
How To Powerize Your Memory

Chapter 4
Taking Notes In Class

Chapter 5
Taking Notes From Texts

Introduction

There is no easy way to become a successful A+ student. While it is true that school work comes easier to some, (let's face it there are those with 180 I.Q.s) the rest of us can also hit the mark. But it takes real effort and drive.

How can we possibly remember all the information that our teachers give us in lectures and that we read in texts? No doubt a daunting task! In recent years research in brain function has helped us to understand better exactly how humans learn and how our memories work.

For example, scientists have identified at least six different long term memory areas where we file information that we perceive. If we know how to access these memory banks, we will be better able to recall the data that we are expected to learn.

This book explains how you can use note taking as a tool to improve your ability to learn and remember the volumes of information you get in lectures and texts. You will learn the basic skills of good note taking that are broken down into specific, easy to remember tasks. With a little practice you can become an A+ student.

The system does require some preparation of your note books in special formats for lecture notes and text notes. However, note book preparation is simple and accomplished in a few minutes.

The rest is up to you. Like the accomplished pianist, low handicap golfer, or top notch athlete, you must decide that you will practice, practice, and practice until the skills of note taking and studying from notes become automatic.

Good luck with your goal of becoming an A+ student!

Part I

What is a Skill?

Understanding Memory Research

How to Powerize Your Memory

Chapter 1

THE SKILL OF NOTE TAKING

WHAT IS A SKILL?

A skill is defined in the American Heritage Dictionary as follows:

1. *Proficiency, facility, or dexterity that is acquired or developed through training or experience.*
2. *An art, trade or technique particularly one requiring the use of hands or body.*
3. *A developed talent or ability: writing skills.*

All through your life you have been developing skills. Just think of all those you have acquired: As a five year old you learned to tie your shoelaces. That was a tough one. Later, you learned to balance your two wheeler without training wheels. Gradually you acquired the myriad skills that make it possible for you to function as an adult. Anything you do that requires you to use your hands or body or senses that needed some training and/or practice to develop minimum proficiency is a skill.

Think of learning to play the piano. How difficult! The beginner must learn to read music and associate the printed notes with the keyboard. The fingers are placed on the keys. Slowly, the brain learns to send messages to the fingers to strike certain keys. Only through regular, spaced practice can anyone become a decent pianist. It is amazing that once the skill becomes embedded, the muscles seem to develop a memory of their own and they easily respond to the brain's messages.

Learning a sports skill is no different. Good tennis players and golfers practice many hours, honing the strokes, creating images in the brain that send messages to muscles that memorize the motions that generate the great tennis serve or the perfect chip, drive, or putt in golf.

Low level skills such as brushing your teeth, tying your shoes, or cutting your steak are easily learned. We are barely aware that they are skills. The tough ones: learning to touch type on a QWERTY keyboard, learning to play a musical instrument, or learning to take notes in class or from a text require sustained effort and practice.

Here are the rules for learning new skills

1.   Break down the skill into its several components. For example, when learning to word process you would identify the components like this:

First component: Learn the "home keys" on which your fingers sit at rest: ASDF for the left hand and JKL; for the right hand.

Second component: Learn the finger muscle motion needed to press the home keys to get a letter on the computer screen.

2. Practice. To master any skill practice is a must. In word processing you must practice the movement needed to type the letters "J" and "F" with the pointer finger of each hand. You must train your finger muscles to strike the keys automatically without thinking or looking down at the keys by building muscle memory. And so you begin, almost child-like, to type FFF - JJJ with the index fingers of your left and right hands respectively. You check to make sure that your hands are at the

correct angle and that the proper pressure and rhythm are used. You watch the computer screen to be sure you are hitting the correct keys.

3.   Drill.   Educational psychologists have learned that frequent, short periods of practice are much more powerful than single, long periods of effort. It is better to practice in three separate ten minute drill sessions spaced during the day than in one thirty minute session. In the long session, fatigue, loss of attention, and distractions detract from the value of the practice. Obviously, the learner must be committed to spending sufficient time for practice and drill to develop mastery of any high level skill.

Where are we going with all this discussion about skills?

THE SKILL OF NOTE TAKING

Believe it or not, note taking is a skill just like playing the piano because it fits the definition of an activity that requires you to use your body and your mind together to allow you to do something automatically and without very much conscious thought. You have been taught many "school" skills, but unfortunately few teachers take the time to teach note taking. Note taking is a skill that must be broken down into its component parts, practiced, and drilled frequently. It is an important skill that is absolutely necessary for success in school.

Researchers have discovered that effective note taking has a high correlation with outstanding school achievement. It should be a major weapon in your arsenal of learning tools.

Note Taking is an Important Skill Because It:

■ Helps raise your grades

■ Helps you summarize lectures and texts

■ Helps you study for tests

■ Forces you to be an active listener and reader

■ Improves your memory

A bit later in this book you will learn how to break note taking down into its component parts and learn how to practice each one. Since it is a relatively high level skill, not unlike piano playing or keyboarding, it will require practice, drill and commitment. One does not become a fine pianist, tennis player, or water colorist without motivation and desire. You will need a healthy supply of these last traits to succeed.

THE RELATIONSHIP BETWEEN NOTE TAKING AND LEARNING

So note taking is an important skill and it is going to improve your grades, help you study for tests, and improve your memory. How will note taking accomplish all this? It will do it because note taking is a skill that facilitates learning. We learn because our brains can remember. We could not learn to play the piano if after diligent, spaced practice sessions with scales we could not remember the notes or remember how to move our fingers. What a waste that would be! All that practice gone! Note taking facilitates learning by helping our brains to remember information.

Many studies have shown the positive effect of note taking on achievement. Note taking helps students to focus while learning and aids students to think through new material more fully. Moreover, as new material is presented in subsequent lectures or readings, note taking helps students link the new information with that previously taught.

HOW DO I KNOW I CAN DO IT?

In case you're thinking that improving study and note taking skills is too tough for you, consider these ideas:

■ Success in school and life is more a matter of will and drive than innate ability. Remember Edison's oft quoted comment, "Genius is ten percent inspiration and ninety percent perspiration."

■ Most people use only a tiny part of their potential. Imagine what you can accomplish if you really get going.

■ Most of us have enough basic intelligence and ability to handle any of today's jobs or professions if we are determined to succeed. We tend to be held back by our own feelings of doubt and some outmoded beliefs.

■ Consider the popular marathon races. The first to come across the finish line and the last have all come the same distance. So it is with school. If you master all the material in a course, you will know just as much as the fastest student in the class. It may simply take you a little longer, but your "A" will be worth just as much.

■ Think of yourself as a winner and you will be one!

■ Winners, people who succeed, set goals for themselves. The most successful set a long range goal and then lay out a series of short term goals designed to carry them along the road to achieving their main objective.

Be a Winner!
Set Your Personal Goals

Here is your Long Term Goal:
I will be successful in school!

Here are your short term goals:

I will use Bud's Easy Note Taking System for two weeks.

I will be able to complete all note taking tasks satisfactorily and feel my skill in note taking growing.

I will become more confident in class and see improvement in class participation and grades.

In the next chapter we will explore what learning theorists have begun to discover about how our brains work and how we remember and actually learn.

Chapter 2
Understanding Memory Research

We go to school to learn. It makes sense for you to understand how scientists believe humans learn. What happens in our brains when we read a textbook, listen to a lecture, or watch an educational film? How do we sort out the important ideas from the unimportant? What can we do to remember the significant material? Why do some people seem to learn more easily than others?

This chapter will explain how we respond to the words and sounds we read or hear and the images we see and how we use them in our attempts to learn new information. By understanding the way your brain processes new data, you will know how to use your brain to help you learn and remember. Let's get started with a basic picture of how our brains work.

Latest Memory Research

Research on how humans respond to information and learn is continually evolving with new theories and hypotheses being tested. While not all scientists agree, there is consensus around the concepts of working memory and long term memory.

WORKING MEMORY

Working memory is where we *consciously* process new stimuli that we receive as images or sounds. We are totally aware of the stimuli. We know that we are receiving sounds and images and we are fully cognizant of our attempts to deal with them.

One function of working memory is to process stimuli in its sensory memory section. Sounds are called echoic stimuli. Echoic stimuli can only be held for seconds in sensory memory before they disappear. An example of an echoic or sound stimuli would be the telephone number a friend gives you. Most people can only hold a phone number in working memory until they finish dialing.

Think of stopping and asking someone on the street for driving directions. "Turn right at the first stop sign, then left at the gas station, then watch for the split and turn half right when you see the burned out house." Unless you repeat the directions several times, you will find it almost impossible to retain them longer than a few seconds.

Visual images are called iconic stimuli. Visual or iconic memory is also retained only for a brief lapse of time. Suppose a photograph were flashed on a screen for five seconds and then removed. If you were asked to describe the photograph, you would have great difficulty remembering more than a few details.

George Miller, a Harvard psychologist, found that humans can only recall 7 plus or minus 2 items in working memory. He called it the Magic 7. For example, suppose you were asked to recall a series of 13 letters such as: FLUSAINNASAUN. You would probably have difficulty. However, if you consciously process the stimuli, you are able to retain visual and auditory stimuli in working memory for longer periods. For example, combining bits of data or "chunking" can make remembering easier. If you "chunked" the 13 letters into 5 chunks like this: FL - USA - IN - NASA - UN you would have much less difficulty. In some ways, working memory operates like RAM in computers.

When we receive stimuli in working memory we hold them a few seconds just long enough to connect with long term memories stored away. As we concentrate on the stimulus received, we activate related long term memories that allow us to solve problems or to take necessary action. For example, if a teacher describes a scientific event such as a lunar eclipse, we will almost instantaneously begin recalling data in long term memory about the sun, the moon, rotation, revolution, light and many other bits of information we have previously stored in long term memory about the solar system and the earth.

Many students "get by" in school by keeping data in working memory just long enough to get it down on a test paper. This is what "cramming" for exams is all about and why it does not work. Try to recall the things you crammed last year. The crammed dates, formulas, and ideas that were only in working memory are gone!

LONG TERM MEMORY

Six Long Term Memory Areas

Brain researchers now believe there are at least six long term memory areas: Procedural, Semantic, Emotional, Episodic, Conditioned Response, and Spatial. Data we receive in working memory may move to one or more of these long term storage areas.

We can store and access a tremendous amount of information in long term memory. It is like the hard drive in your computer with the difference that your long term memory brain "drive" has an enormous, perhaps unlimited capacity. We are constantly moving data from our working memory to our long term memory area.

Some data become permanently stored in long term memory without any conscious help from us. For example, most people cannot get the picture of the World Trade Center buildings collapsing out of their minds. Other information that we would love to make permanent such as some mathematical equations, chemical formulas, or historical events just don't seem to stick for most of us.

Your goal in reading this book is to learn how to make information in your long term memory as permanent as you can. You want to be able to recall it for tests or to use it to carry out functions. This chapter and the next will give you important suggestions for improving your long term memory!

Procedural Memory

Any physical action that uses a combination of mental activity (reading sheet music and sending messages through the nerves to the fingers) and physical activity (striking piano keys) that we can do without thinking comes from the procedural memory part of long term memory.

Driving a car, playing tennis, painting, and playing a guitar are clear examples of procedures in which muscles spontaneously respond to mental stimuli. This is where all of our learned skills are stored. You have already mastered thousands of such procedures or skills. You are working now to get the skill of note taking embedded in your procedural memory!

The beginning guitar player must think very consciously about what he or she is doing. The learner must look at the music, visually check the location of the strings, carefully place the fingers, and then probably look up at the music again before actually strumming the guitar. This is the way you slowly and painstakingly begin to learn new procedures or skills. Only after considerable and regular practice can the seasoned acoustic guitarist play well without conscious thought. The more the guitarist practices, the more automatic her skill becomes, and the more beautiful the music!

Procedural Memory and Note Taking

Because note taking will be the foundation for building your long term memory of texts and lectures, you should understand the similarity of note taking to keyboarding or piano playing. Procedural memories become increasingly more deeply embedded as you practice the new skills. Think of how much more confidence you had as a bike rider after a few years of riding compared with your early first attempts to balance without training wheels. You can now ride with one hand and talk at the same time!

Your ability to take notes spontaneously without conscious thought will improve rapidly with practice. You have many opportunities to practice every time you are in a class listening to a lecture or reading a text so your skill should improve very quickly. Before long you will be taking notes and studying almost without thinking. Your skill level will continue to improve and you will gradually take notes more fully, more quickly, and more efficiently! Chapter 3 will provide detailed instructions for building the procedural memory of note taking!

Studying, Learning, and Long Term Memory

Before you begin learning to build your long term procedural memory of note taking, let's explore the latest research in the other five long term memory areas.

Semantic Memory

This is the big kahuna of them all because semantic information is language information. Our semantic memory is filled with things we "know" intuitively. For example, we "know" that paint comes in many colors. We "know" that fish are vertebrates.

Words and images are the source of our "knowing." In school situations we are constantly listening to lectures in class and reading from texts to enlarge our knowledge base. Gradually, our semantic memory grows as we come to "know" more and more. Unfortunately, much of the knowledge we receive will gradually fade from our long term memory unless we take specific steps to embed it deeply

Information, data, concepts, and general understandings that are not connected to a specific event such as an accident or hospital stay make up much of our semantic memory. Concepts related to specific events are stored in episodic memory and may also be embedded in emotional memory.

Our problem is to recall at will the specific knowledge that we need at a particular moment from the immense hard drive of our long term memory. We need to recall dates, formulas, concepts, and ideas to take action demanded by a new stimulus received in working memory. Frequently, the immediate stimulus is a question on a quarterly examination in one of your school classes. Our working memory is stimulated by the reading of the test question. Immediately synapses form to reach into your long term memory for the knowledge needed to answer the question. The most frequently tested and graded stuff is the data in your long term semantic memory.

When working memory stimuli (the question on the exam) call for the information in long term memory, you will not be able to recall it if the data has not been laid down in strong, clear, powerful terms. Information received in long term semantic memory must be be kneaded, squeezed, stretched and frequently reinforced to make sure it sticks. In the next chapter we will explore some techniques for processing data in long term memory so it can be easily recalled. But first, let's look at the other long term memory storage areas. Some of them can help reinforce data in our semantic memory.

Emotional Memory

During an emotional experience we lay down very strong, clear traces in our long term emotional memory. David Goleman, a researcher, believes that this is the most powerful of all the memory areas. Some images, like the World Trade Center attack or the funeral of a loved one, are transferred almost immediately to your long term emotional memory bank. Data accompanied by fear, sadness, joy, anger, or other strong emotions tend to be firmly and permanently implanted in this powerful, long term memory area.

Unfortunately, a strong emotion like fear can trigger the "flight or fight" response. The adrenalin rush that prepares the body can short circuit access to other memory areas. Panic deprives us of the ability to think clearly and to call up important information stored in long term memory. Even those trained to deal with emergency situations sometimes find that they cannot recall the proper actions to take to save their own lives.

Emotions can also wreak havoc in test situations. Have you ever opened a test booklet, glanced at the questions, felt overwhelmed by the scope of the test, and found that your mind had gone blank. Information firmly stored in long term memory was suddenly inaccessible.

Episodic Memory

When we remember events, the times and places they occurred, and anything we learned during the event we are plumbing our episodic memory. Once you have experienced an event or episode, it is stored and the data surrounding the event can be easily recalled. Your recollection of the World Trade Center attack is an example of a deeply and strongly embedded episodic memory.

Episodic memories can change and embellish semantic memories. For example, our semantic memory tells us that we "know" what hospitals are and how they work. However, after a personal hospital stay, your semantic knowledge of hospitals will change as the events of the episode filter down into your long term memory.

Sometimes episodic memory colors our emotional memory. Episodes that are highly emotional such as an accident, an illness, or a death in the family will likely be more easily and vividly remembered than events that are more benign.

Conditioned Response Memory

You have probably heard of the famous scientist, Pavlov, who rang a bell every time a dog was fed. After a few trials, the dog would salivate when the bell was rung even though no food was offered. The stimulus of the bell ringing caused the automatic response of salivation. This is called a conditioned response. Conditioning requires either a reward or a punishment accompanying a behavior for the conditioning to take place.

The researcher, E. Jensen, found that we learn many conditioned or automatic responses as we grow and learn. When we gain approval or satisfaction following an activity, we gradually build a conditioned response to the activity. There is a huge quantity of data in your conditioned response long term memory. All the addition, subtraction, multiplication, and division facts (2+6=8, 4-6=2, 2x9=18, etc.) that you learned in elementary school using flash cards and drills are there. Many of the songs you learned over the years are buried in your conditioned response memory. You hear the first few bars of a melody and immediately the entire song pours out. The reading cues you use to decode words through their initial consonants or their shapes are all in your conditioned response memory.

Conditioned response memory and procedural memory are somewhat inter-related. Much of what we use in procedural memory may be partly a conditioned response as when we respond to musical cues.

Spatial or Locational Memory

Spatial memory is what we develop as we form images of our location in space. For example, if you had to enter your bedroom at night during a blackout, you could probably navigate fairly well without bumping into furniture. You had in your spatial memory bank the location and distances of the furniture and other articles in the room.

Spatial memory also allows us to follow directions. If you arrived at an airport in a strange city, your spatial memory would enable you to reach a destination by responding to specific directions: "Go to the first traffic light, turn left, go three miles until you reach a MacDonalds on your right, turn left at that intersection, go a half mile and you will see the entrance to the campus on your right." Spatial memory gives us a sense of where we are in space. We "know" left from right, we can judge distances, and recognize landmarks.

Summary

Now that you understand how our memory works, it is easy to see that if you remember something you have learned it. If you remember how to tie your shoes, you have learned how to tie your shoes. If you remember how to solve an equation, you have learned how to solve an equation. If you remember how to play a scale, you have learned how to play a scale.

So what is important in learning is strengthening memory. In the next chapter you will learn how to do just that. And the primary tool for improving and strengthening your memory will be note taking!

Here is the most important equation in education:

Remembering = Learning

Chapter 3

How To Powerize Your Memory

BUILDING PROCEDURAL MEMORY

■ Practice, Practice, Practice

Your goal is to make note taking an automatic, unconscious skill like driving or playing an instrument. Here is the bad news. Regular intensive practice is required. There is no other way. If you studied an instrument as a youngster, you probably remember your mother constantly imploring you to practice. If you persisted you are now an accomplished musician. If you faltered, no doubt you have abandoned your instrument, or at best can haltingly play a few favorites.

So it is with developing the procedural memory required for note taking. You are reading this book because you want to learn how to take great notes in class and from texts. Because note taking is a skill that is built on procedural memory, you will have to devote time to learn and practice the steps of note taking.

Even a great athlete like Tiger Woods spends hours each week practicing, perfecting each challenging stroke in golf. Golf pros hits hundreds of balls every day. Concert musicians spend hours each day practicing and playing in an effort to perfect their performances. The great athletes and musicians of the world are great not only because they have talent. They also have the motivation and drive to be the best. And they can only achieve the heights by constant practice.

If you really want to be a big league student, you must commit to regular practice. If you are motivated to become an A+ student, you will do what it takes and do it with enthusiasm. All it takes is **PRACTICE, PRACTICE, PRACTICE!**

BUILDING SEMANTIC MEMORY

Long term semantic memory can be enhanced using the techniques that follow:

■ Identify the main ideas of all new data.

Identify the major concepts. Be aware that of the many words you hear or see when receiving new information only a few represent the main ideas. The rest are subordinate ideas, examples, illustrations, or comparisons. Try to learn the difference. You must separate the main ideas from the rest and imprint a few strong, clear images of those ideas in your semantic memory. For example, as you jot down data, ask yourself: Is this the main idea? Is this a supporting part of the main idea? Is this an example? An illustration? A comparison?

■ Analyze information you are storing

Analyzing and thinking about information helps to develop deeper memory traces. As you turn ideas over in your mind, you develop personal ownership of them. Asking yourself questions about new data is a method of analysis. How is this subject related to what you learned yesterday? How does the new information compare with other ideas you have? How does it contrast? The more you analyze, the easier it will be for you to recall the information.

As you take notes underline or highlight the main ideas but not the supporting ideas, illustrations, or examples. Think about how the main ideas relate to examples.

You can get help identifying main ideas in texts and lectures. Bold headings in texts and underlined words on white boards in class signify main ideas. Teachers may even call attention to important ideas by statements, using colored markers, or just by a change in voice. If you hear, "This is one of the most important concepts to remember," you've heard a main idea.

The brain cannot remember all the details of an hour long lecture, but it can hold the main concepts if you consciously reduce what you have heard to only the most important ideas and lay down strong, powerful, clear memory traces. If you do not break the new data down into its main ideas, the brain receives a large blur of information that will be virtually impossible to recall.

■ Add new data to an "advance organizer" or organizational framework that already exists in your memory.

We have imprinted in our semantic memories a kind of outline or advance organizer of each of the subjects we have learned over the years. For example, we have studied history, science, literature, mathematics, and many other subjects. For each of these subjects we have a general framework embedded in our semantic memories. We study American history several times during a school career. Each repetition adds new information to the existing framework built by the earlier learnings. For example, during a college lecture on Reconstruction, we recall, almost sub-consciously, what we learned in high school of the Civil War and its aftermath . Each time we receive new information it finds its place on the already existing framework and it "sticks." As you do advanced study try to recall the older learnings and see where the new knowledge fits on the existing framework you have already stored.

Handouts or outlines distributed by many teachers before a lecture serve as advance organizers. Study these carefully. You can see the entire scope of the lecture before it begins. As the lecture continues, think about how the new information you are receiving fits on the total framework. Instead of isolated data, you can see how the various parts of the lecture relate to each other. The teacher's outline gives your brain a framework on which to attach new facts as they are received.

Prepare your own advance organizer or outline when taking notes from a text. Look through the table of contents to get an overview. Scan the chapter for bold face paragraph headings. Make a written outline using the major headings and sub-headings of the chapter before you begin reading.

Try to see the whole picture of the chapter before you read it. Recite the major topics. Can you see how they relate to each other? Recite the outline from memory. Later, as you read intensively, you will know the general framework of the whole chapter and understand how each section fits into the whole scheme. You will be attaching new information to the framework of the outline.

Learning a theory, law, or principle before reading or hearing about examples or supporting ideas also serves as an advance organizer. Because you know the law or theory, you will better understand how the example or supporting idea relates to the theory and how it fits on the framework of the theory. For example, in economics the law of diminishing returns states that at some point each additional unit of input yields less and less output. If you learned the law first, it would be easy for you to understand what was happening if a small chain of three retail clothing shops in a small city added a fourth and found that the chain's total sales dropped.

■ Review recently learned material just before hearing or reading new related information.

Reviewing ties the new data to the existing data. Reviewing helps lay down a strong, clear trace of the new data in semantic memory by joining it to earlier learnings. Suppose you are studying an historical trend such as the rise of democracy in a developing country. Imagine that during a lecture on Monday you learned two events: the rise of an intellectual movement and the growth of an entrepreneurial class. By reviewing those events just before Wednesday's lecture, you reinforce the original memory of the growing democratic trends. You are then ready to tie on the new event, the fall of a military junta, you are about to hear about on Wednesday. By tying the learnings of the two lectures together, you build a strong memory trace of the overall three event trend.

You can do the same with texts. Review the contents of a previous chapter before reading the next chapter. This will help join the new information to the earlier and will reinforce the total semantic memory.

■ Reduce ideas to symbols, maps, diagrams, and pictures.

Transform newly analyzed data into symbolic language. This requires higher order thinking and gives you ownership of the data by transforming the original concept into a symbol of your own making. For example, if you were taking notes on the westward expansion of the United States, you might draw a little sombrero to represent Mexican trade next to the notes you wrote. You don't have to be an artist. Anything you draw that looks at all like the symbol will be fine. These symbols are easy to remember and will help you to recall the full information later.

Example of data transformed into a symbol

Word "maps" make it easy to remember concepts. When trying to learn a complicated concept, analyze the main ideas and supporting ideas and arrange them in a map. Think of how the ideas relate to each other. Join the main topics and supporting words or phrases with lines to show the relationships among them. Enclose each word or phrase in a circle or oval.

Example of a word "map" showing relationships among ideas

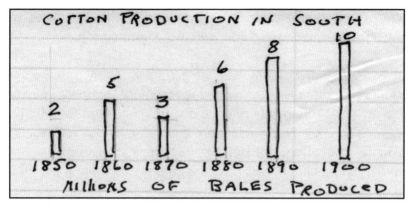

Example of a graph describing data

Draw diagrams, graphs, and charts. You can more easily internalize and store a diagram in your long term memory than a written description of the same data. Analyze the data and design a diagram, chart, or graph that best illustrates the concept. Planning the diagram or chart forces you to visualize the data. Drawing the diagram, graph or chart heavily reinforces the strong, clear memory trace you are laying down. It will be easy to recall the data from your semantic memory.

■ Arrange ideas in groups or "chunks"

Look for common elements to group ideas when presented with a great deal of information. Remember the rule of seven. You normally can hold five plus or minus two bits of information in short term memory for just a few seconds. If you are presented with lots of data, try to arrange them in easily recognizable "chunks.

For example, if you are studying the Middle East you will read and hear much about the various countries, their many religions and unusual relationships to say nothing of their rich histories. To top it off, your Western mind is unfamiliar with the culture and the languages so you will not have much of an advance organizer as you do with more familiar topics.

Chunking is one way of getting difficult information from short term memory to semantic memory. Suppose you are having trouble remembering the major countries of the Middle East. There are eight - one more than the magic seven: Saudi Arabia, Iran, Iraq, Jordan, Israel, Afghanistan, Turkey, and Syria. If you chunk them into two groups of three and five like this you will remember them easily. [Israel, Iran, Iraq] [Jordan, Afghanistan, Syria, Saudia Arabia, Turkey] to form the acronym: I I I   J A S S T.

You can do the same with the various religions, tribes, and conflicts and with any other difficult to remember data.

Example of notes arranged in "chunks"

■ Summarize information using the original language.

Summarizing calls on us to think carefully about the new information, digest it, and reduce it to its shortest version using the language of the original text. It is a powerful technique because it requires higher order thinking skills.

■ Paraphrase information using your own words.

Paraphrasing is an even more powerful tool than summarizing for laying down strong, clear memory traces in semantic memory. This process cooks the ideas in the stew of your personal past experiences. When ideas are re-phrased in your own words, you have a sense of ownership of them and they are easier to recall. Paraphrasing calls on higher order thinking skills. This technique may also connect feelings about the new data you stored in your emotional long term memory thereby reinforcing the new semantic memory.

■ Write a test question.

Write the most thought provoking, hard questions about the new information by beginning with the words, how, why, and explain. Easier questions begin with the words, list, who, what, when, state, identify, define and describe. By phrasing questions you are reorganizing the data and digesting it. Writing questions helps cement the information in your semantic memory. Answering your own questions is even better!

■ *Prepare a time line.*

Timelines provide a strong, visual, symbolic representation of the events in historical sequence. By using scale to represent the passage of years, you help your brain absorb and hold difficult data. Include symbols above the dates to further reinforce the events in your semantic memory. A crown for a king or an ax to portray an ancient battle will do. See the illustration on the following page for an example of a student's timeline.

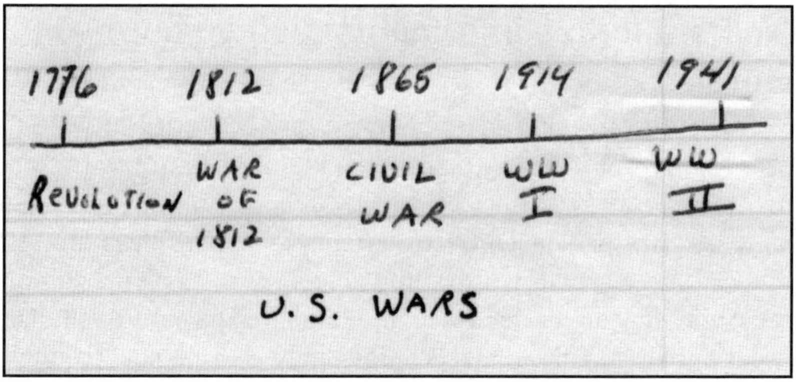
1776
1812
1865
1914
1941
REVOLUTION
WAR OF 1812
CIVIL WAR
WW I
WW II
U.S. WARS

Example of a timeline to represent historical events

Use mnemonics.

Write acronyms. Acronyms are groups of letters formed from the first letters of a group of words to help us remember. Our language is filled with acronyms that often are used instead of the actual words they represent. RADAR for Radio Detection and Ranging, FBI for Federal Bureau of Investigation, NASA for National Aeronautics and Space Administration, and FAQ for Frequently Asked Questions are common acronyms.

You can invent your own acronyms for words or data you want to recall easily. Here is an example. Heard of Roy G. Biv? That's the acronym for the colors of the spectrum: red, orange, yellow, green, blue, indigo, and violet. Suppose you want to recall the major elements that make up our long term memory. They are emotional, conditioned response, procedural, semantic, episodic, and spatial. Use the first letters of each word, ECPSES, and rearrange them so they form an acronym that is easy for you to remember. For example, SEPECS might be good for you or SPEECS might be better.

Be aware that acronyms only serve to jog rote memory. They do not help with comprehension. Moreover, not every data series will lend itself to the formation of acronyms. Too many acronyms to remember can cause more problems than you need, so limit them to the concepts that are most important.

Write acrostics. Acrostics are sentences formed from the first letters of words you want to remember. Acrostics have been used for centuries as tricks of language and as mnemonic devices. Instead of forming a single word as in acronyms, you create a whole sentence.

Remember this acrostic sentence for the musical scale? Every Good Boy Does Fine stands for the musical notes, EGBDF. Medical students have a host of acrostics to remember the physiology of the human body. Here is one for the bones of the skull. Old People From Texas Eat Spiders for Occipital, Parietal, Frontal, Temporal, Ethmoid, and Sphenoid.

If you want to remember several items, list them and try to make a sentence using the first letters of each item. You can make up an acrostic for the main ideas of an important lecture or the main parts of a book chapter.

■ *Use word and image association*

Associate words with freaky images. Memory experts suggest associating new ideas that you want to remember with words or images that you know. Selecting silly or unusual links is a good technique.

Suppose you have trouble recalling the names of some of Abraham Lincoln's cabinet members. They were William Henry Seward, Secretary of State; Salmon P. Chase, Secretary of the Treasury; and Edward Bates, Attorney General.

Look at each name and link a word picture to it. These are easy. Seward sounds like sewer. Salmon is a fish and there is a chase there, too. Bates sounds like bait. Would the following help? Edward used bait to chase salmon in Henry's sewer. You can use this technique in many situations. The quirkier your links, the more effective it will be.

■ *Recite in your own words.*

Recitation is one of the most powerful of all the tools for getting data deeply into long term semantic memory! Because reciting involves the use of your vocal and hearing nerves and muscles, you will be adding layers of memory.

After you have mastered information, recite it aloud in your own words. In order to do this you must have fully digested the material. By using your own words you have taken ownership of the material. The information is no longer just notes in the words of your teacher or of the text writer. You have chewed, swallowed, and digested the data. It is now your own!

How often should you recite? Once is not enough! You should recite the information periodically in order to reinforce that clear, accurate, powerful memory trace. Every time you recite it is as if you are driving a car over the same tracks in a soft, grass field. The more often you do it, the deeper the tracks.

Reciting is difficult, but the more repetitions you make, the better you will be able to recall data when you need it to answer an examination question!

■ Teach the material.

Teaching is one step above recitation. In order to

teach you must have fully integrated the data or information into your long term memory.

You will have absorbed and digested the information and reformulated it in your mind. By teaching the information you are once again recalling and reciting the data. When you recall, you must reconstruct the information.

If you have a group of friends who study with you, agree to have each of you teach the material. As you prepare your lecture you may find that you are not so sure about parts. You will have to review those areas and improve your plan.

Good teachers are prepared for questions from their students. Encourage your study mates to challenge you with questions. You may discover more areas that need beefing up.

BUILDING EMOTIONAL MEMORY
■ Relate the data to your personal life.
Get information into your emotional memory area. If you can do it, you will have two long term areas to draw upon. The emotional memory will reinforce the semantic memory.

The trick in studying is to try to find a way to relate what we have learned to our personal lives. People who love baseball can remember the batting averages of dozens of players. Stock market traders can recall the stock symbols and prices of many companies. It is their intense motivation or emotional attachment that makes this possible. Most of us can remember more trivia about our hobbies than we can about school work because of our deep, personal interest. Try to develop a real interest in the subject you are learning and you will find yourself remembering more.

In the social studies area you may try to imagine yourself as a character. How would you have felt in Lincoln's shoes as he prepared the Gettysburg Address? You might try to become emotionally involved by imagining yourself debating an issue.

Try to think of other ways that the new material relates to your own life. Can this scientific discovery have an effect on you and your offspring? How will it affect the way we live?

If you believe the learning will be helpful to you or has some other emotional element, you will remember it more easily. Linking the new learning to some emotional event in your life is also helpful.

For example, if you are studying a play in English class, perhaps you can tie the learning to an experience you had acting in a school production. Learning about nativism and the Know Nothing Party in U.S. history may evoke an emotional reaction as you think of your feelings about the current immigration debates dealing with illegal aliens. You will access the new data through your emotional memory as well as your semantic memory.

BUILDING EPISODIC MEMORY

Episodic memory rarely needs beefing up. The events are usually so powerful that they remain in memory for quite a long time, especially because they are often linked with emotional experience. However, if an episode or event is related to something you are learning, it is worthwhile to take a few moments to reflect on the original episode and how it may impact on the new learning. For example, if you have a strong memory of a very positive episode in a former history class when the teacher heavily praised your work, you might reinforce that memory and tie it to the lecture in the current class.

BUILDING CONDITIONED RESPONSE MEMORY

■ Drill

Drills build conditioned responses. Old fashioned drills are what built your conditioned responses to number facts. Use 3 x 5 inch cards. Write important information such as new vocabulary, dates, and events on one side and the clues on the other. Carry them with you and when you have a minute, take them out and drill yourself.

■ Use Songs

Use a song melody to reinforce conditioned responses. Do you remember how you first learned to recite the alphabet as a child? You sang it to the tune of "Twinkle Twinkle Little Star." Think of all the song lyrics you can sing in the shower. If you hear just the first few bars of music, you can probably sing all the words of the entire song. Songs and rhymes slip easily into long term memory and are very easy to recall. Think of all the songs, poems, and rhymes that you can recite almost at will.

Making up lyrics using the concepts you want to learn to fit an old tune can build a powerful, clear trace deep in long term memory. If you are good at writing musical parodies to old tunes, this may be an excellent way to get data into conditioned response memory. Try using popular "raps" as a basis. Just fit in the words or phrases that you want to remember.

Perhaps you and some friends might make this part of a study session. Reciting the new rhyme or singing the new lyric a few times will make recall of the new data very easy. And it might be fun!

BUILDING SPATIAL MEMORY

Spatial memory, like episodic memory, has been built over time to give you clear knowledge of boundaries and the ability to navigate the environment. As you mature so does your spatial memory and your ability to understand relative distances and directions and to fully understand your relationship to your environment. If you are taking courses in architecture or engineering your spatial memory will continue to improve.

BUD'S NOTE TAKING SYSTEM FIGHTS FORGETTING

Bud's Note Taking System is a prescription against forgetting. As you use the techniques, you will find that every sub-skill of note taking is based on the brain research about memory described above. Above all, make Bud's Note Taking System a regular part of your study habits.

Part II

How To Take Great Notes In Class

How To Take Great Notes From Texts

Chapter 4
Taking Notes in Class

You are now ready to begin training to be a champion note taker. Just as the olympic swimmer or skier trains, be prepared for some intensive work. If you ever learned to play a musical instrument, you will understand the steps you need to take to develop proficiency. Note taking is a skill that requires procedural memory training along the same lines as learning to play an instrument or to paint landscapes. You must break the skill into its component parts, learn them, and practice, practice, practice.

It's not a good idea to try to learn a new skill in actual competition, so we will begin by setting up some training exercises.

Select A Training Site and Equipment

Concert pianists don't immediately go on stage in Carnegie Hall and competitive sprinters don't just dash out and compete on the track. Athletes set up a training schedule of practice at a gym, practice room, or track. You, as a neophyte note taker, must do the same. While you will not need the special track shoes, stop watch, athletic clothing or time at a practice track, you will need a few simple things to get started.

How do these sound?

Your Note Taking Training Equipment
Blue and red ball point pens and a highlighter.
A reasonably comfortable chair and desk.
Your notebook with several pages prepared as shown on pages 4-4 and 4-5.
A quiet room with a TV.

Your Note Taking Training Site

Avoid sitting on a sofa. Set up a small table with a straight chair in front of a tv set to simulate a classroom setting.

Training With TV Programs

Now you need someone to give a lecture so you can begin learning to take notes! Guess what? Almost all day and night people are "lecturing" on TV! It is a perfect practice venue. Check the TV listings to find interesting C-Span, History and Discovery Channel programs. Look for public TV specials and political speeches. You might even choose some programs you have absolutely no interest in because that is a situation you will probably face in school. In a pinch you can use regular news broadcasts, although these are usually too short to be good for training.

Plan a TV Training Schedule.

Short, spaced practices are better than one long session. Plan a schedule of 3 daily spaced sessions of only 5 to 10 minute lengths for a week. Try for an early morning, mid-day, and evening session each day.

Complete all 8 tasks described in this chapter for every session.

Tape Recording or Using Real Shorthand?

Tape recording is OK in a regular classroom (if allowed) but only to check on points you feel you may have missed. Listening to a recorded lecture takes as long as the original and you still have to take notes.

If you have been trained in real shorthand, use it only to take notes. Transcribing a full lecture is a waste of time and not as good as note taking.

Academic note taking requires you to set up your notebook in a special way. This system was developed at Cornell University some years ago. While it may seem to take some time initially, you will find the preparation simple.

HOW TO PREPARE YOUR NOTEBOOK

LEFT HAND PAGE

Top line: **Course Name**   **Topic**   **Date**

Second line: **Next Reading Assignment**

Draw a Horizontal Line Across the Middle of the Page

Label Top Section: **Maps, Diagrams, Timelines**

Draw Two More Horizontal Lines dividing the lower half of the page into three sections.

Label Top Section: **Lecture Organization**

Label Middle Section: **Personal Statement**

Label Bottom Section: **Possible Exam Question**

RIGHT HAND AND FOLLOWING PAGES

Top line: **Course Name**   **Topic**   **Date**

Rule a vertical line two inches from the left edge

Label Right Column: **Full Lecture Notes**

Label Left Column: **Personal Restatement**

See the Sample Pages on 4-4 and 4-5.

Sample Left Hand Page

COURSE NAME   LECTURE TOPIC   DATE
FUTURE ASSIGNMENT:
         MAPS   DIAGRAMS   TIME LINES

LECTURE ORGANIZATION

PERSONAL STATEMENT

POSSIBLE EXAM
QUESTION

THE LEFT HAND PAGE SHOULD LIKE THE ONE ABOVE

Sample Right Hand Page

COURSE NAME   Lecture Topic   DATE

PERSONAL   Full   LECTURE   NOTES
RESTATEMENT

THE RIGHT HAND PAGE SHOULD LIKE THE ONE ABOVE

Should You Use Your Computer To Take Notes In Class?

OK, you're a tech junkie. You have an iPod, a Blackberry PDA, and a classy laptop. Microsoft's OneNote and WordPerfect's Lightning are proclaimed as terrific note taking software. There are even new Tablet PCs that use a stylus to capture handwriting. So, should you use your computer to take notes in class?

According to Nigel Ward, a computer professor at the University of Texas, "the short answer is probably not," although, there are some advantages in computer note taking. Your notes could be more legible, more organized, and, as Ward says, you will impress your friends. The negatives are more work and computer demands that will make it hard to stay tuned to the lecture. OneNote and Lightning are designed for business users who have note taking needs that are markedly different from those of students. So for now, we'll say, "No!"

Note Taking Skill Components

What follows are the components of the skill of note taking. When we take a golf lesson, the pro shows us the correct stance, the grip, the backswing, and follow through. Slowly, we try to get all these components into our brains. We set our feet, check to see that our hands are properly placed on the club shaft, watch as we slowly start the backswing. And then, the moment of truth. We are about to hit the ball. We swing hard and we --- miss the ball completely!

This is how we learn new skills. At first we are not very successful, but by diligent and motivated practice, we can make the skill occur spontaneously. We can master golf and guitar playing, and we can become star quality note takers!

Here, then, are the stance, grip, backswing, and follow through of note taking:

Task 1: Take Notes

WHAT BRAIN RESEARCH SAYS
If you are interested and motivated, new data will go to emotional and semantic memory. Strong visual and oral cues create clear, powerful memory traces.

■ DEVELOP A PERSONAL SHORTHAND

1. Shorten words: info for information, def for definition, gov for government, etc.

2. Use symbols: = for equals   + for plus
   > for greater than   < for less than
   w/ for with   w/o for without
   vs for against   sm for small
   lg for large   s/b for should be
   b/4 for before   i.e. for that is
   vs for against   e.g. for for example
   b/c for because   c.f. for compare

3. Omit short, unimportant words like a, the, and adjectives.

4. Use scientific symbols in math and science lectures.

5. Invent your own symbols and shorthand. For example, you can eliminate vowels in many words so a note might look like the illustration on the next page

---

Suppose you heard during a lecture on the Treaty of Versaille: "The Ottoman Empire lost territory." You might write in your new shorthand what you see below:

ottmn Mpe. lst lnd

Example of personal shorthand: Some vowels removed

■ LOOK FOR ADVANCE ORGANIZERS

In regular classes teachers sometimes distribute handouts, outlines, diagrams, and maps before the lecture. These are powerful advance organizers. Always file them with your own notes. While they will not be available during your TV training, be sure to look for them in class. Study them quickly before the class lecture begins.

■ LISTEN ACTIVELY

1. Maintain eye contact with the speaker even though in practice TV sessions you are looking at a screen. Sit up. Concentrate. Show that you are interested.

2. Challenge the speaker silently with questions. Force yourself to be interested.

3. Don't say the lecture is boring.

4. Don't judge or react to the speaker's style, delivery, or dress.

■ WRITE AS FAST AS YOU CAN ON THE RIGHT HAND PAGE

1. Write as legibly as you can. Fast writing is an important note taking component. It will require practice. Be ready to get as much down as possible, but you don't want to write every word the speaker utters.

2. Listen. Then write the main points. Write in simple outline form using phrases, words, or brief sentences in your "shorthand" abbreviations. Break the data down into small pieces or "chunks" that can move from working to long term memory.

■ LISTEN FOR ORAL CUES

1. Listen for cue words like "important," "law", "theory," "effects," "summary," "main points," "outline," "causes," "conclusions," and "remember this." These signal important stuff. Get ideas associated with these cue words down in your notes.

2. Listen for pauses, repetition, changes in pitch, rate and volume of speech. These let you know the speaker is emphasizing an important point. Be sure to copy data associated with these speech patterns.

■ LOOK FOR VISUAL CUES

Look for underlined words or phrases and use of colored chalk or markers on white or black boards or in Power Point presentations. Teachers emphasize important ideas this way.

■ DRAW DIAGRAMS, MAPS, AND TIMELINES IN THE TOP SECTION OF THE FIRST LEFT HAND PAGE

Copy any diagrams or maps or timelines at the top of the left hand page. You can go to an atlas later to clean up a map's accuracy. Make your own timeline after the lecture if the speaker does not draw one.

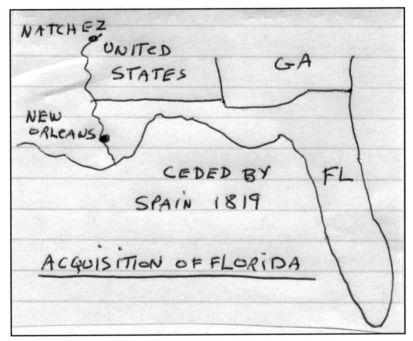

Illustration of a map drawn on left hand page

■ REVIEW YOUR NOTES OF THE PRECEDING RELATED LECTURE BEFORE ATTENDING THIS CLASS

This step will help you tie what you are about to hear to that which you have already incorporated into your long term memory. Do this only if the two lectures are actually related.

Task 2: Read Your Notes

You have almost mastered the first component of note taking. You can listen actively, absorb what you are hearing, and write quickly. Now that you have your notes down on paper, you must begin the process of getting the information and data from your short term memory into your long term memory bank.

■ READ NOTES NO LATER THAN SIX HOURS AFTER THE LECTURE.

1. Read your notes as soon as possible after the lecture. Forgetting begins very quickly.

2. Read your TV practice notes a few hours after viewing to simulate the time lapse (lunch or an intervening class) that normally occurs after a class lecture.

■ CLEAN UP ILLEGIBLE SCRIBBLES

1. Scratch out the illegible words and rewrite them clearly.

2 Do not rewrite your notes totally. It simply takes too long and is not worth the effort. The idea in note taking is to to the job well enough the first time.

■ UNDERLINE OR HIGHLIGHT MAIN IDEAS

1. Separate main ideas from examples.

2. Underline or highlight main ideas but not examples.

Illustration of underlined main ideas and examples not underlined

■ REDUCE THE LECTURE TO A FEW STRONG, CLEAR IDEAS

1. Scan the whole right hand page of your notes.

2. Try to recall the underlined or highlighted main ideas without looking at your notes.

3. Look back at your notes to see how successful you were in recalling the main ideas.

4. Continue until you can recall all the main ideas without looking at your notes. You are laying down strong, clear traces in your long term memory.

Task 3: Restate the Main Ideas In Your Own Words

WHAT BRAIN RESEARCH SAYS

Semantic memory is enhanced when you absorb ideas, mentally digest them, and rephrase them. Symbols and pictures create an easy to remember picture in the brain that is associated with the original information.

■ RE-PHRASE THE FIRST MAIN IDEA OF THE LECTURE

1. Think of a single word or phrase that summarizes the first main idea. Write that single word or phrase in the personal restatement column on the left side of the right hand page.

2. Draw a representative symbol next to the restatement For example, in a lecture on the use of corn to make ethanol you learned: "Corn is good source for ethanol production." You re-phrased it as: "Corn = ethanol." You might draw an ear of corn and a can like this:

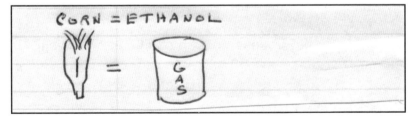

Illustration of a symbol added to re-phrased main idea

3. Continue re-phrasing and drawing symbols for each main idea.

Task 4: Recite Notes Based On Your Restatements

■ BEGIN RECITING

1. Cover the right side of the right hand page. Leave the Personal Restatement column exposed.

2. Look at the first restatement on the left side of the page. Recite aloud, in your own words, as much as you can of the full lecture notes of your first restatement.

3. Uncover your notes and check to see how much you were able to recite.

4. Repeat as necessary until you can recite most of the full lecture notes of the first restatement.

5. Continue the process through each section of your notes.

Task 5: Identify the Lecture's Organizational Pattern.

All lectures are (or at least should be) organized in some pattern. A lecturer discussing World War II might give a chronological view of the events or she might talk about the causes of the war. Another speaker might compare the results of WW I with those of WW II.

Now that you have finished the first four tasks, you are ready to review the entire lecture and decide what organizational pattern the lecturer used. By trying to identify the organizational pattern you are re-thinking all the data and seeing how it hangs together.

■ **ANALYZE ALL THE MAJOR WORDS AND PHRASES YOU WROTE IN THE *PERSONAL RESTATEMENT COLUMN.***

1. Answer questions like the following to help find the organizational pattern.

   How did the lecture begin? How did it end?
   Was the lecture a series of ideas in sequence?
   Did it compare two or more ideas?
   Did it show cause and effect?
   What seemed to be the major theme?

2. Select from the list below the name of the organizational pattern of the lecture.

→ Sequential   → Trend
→ Chronological   → Cause & Effect
→ Categorical   → Comparison
→ Analytical   → Other

■ WRITE A SUMMARY STATEMENT NAMING THE ORGANIZATIONAL PATTERN

1. Think through the answers to the questions above.

2. Write the statement on the left page in the lecture organization section.

Example of a summary organizational pattern statement

■ RECITE THE ORGANIZATIONAL STATEMENT ALOUD

1. Say aloud the statement you wrote describing the organizational pattern.

2. Think of the elements of the lecture as you repeat the statement. In this example, you would think of the comparison of the arguments of the opposing groups. If there had been a cause and effect organization, you would think of the causes and the effects of the topics discussed in the lecture.

Task 6: Relate The Lecture To Your Own Life.

Even scientific data can evoke strong emotions. Studies of cancer research, for example can be related to personal experiences. Historical events, even those centuries old, can be related to your current belief systems. Literature can easily stoke a powerful, personal reaction.

■ ASK YOURSELF, ALOUD, A SERIES OF QUESTIONS THAT RELATE TO YOUR OWN EXPERIENCES.

Ask the following or similar questions.

What emotions do these ideas evoke in me? Do they make me angry, sad, upset?

Does the information remind me of any emotional event in my life? What was it? How are these ideas related to that event?

Have similar thoughts ever occurred to me? What are they?

Do I agree or disagree strongly? Why?
Do the ideas make me think of other questions?

Have I observed or experienced situations myself?

■ WRITE YOUR ANSWERS TO THESE QUESTIONS, OR YOUR OPINIONS AND REACTIONS ON THE LEFT PAGE IN THE PERSONAL STATEMENT SECTION.

> I was upset by the "White Man's Burden" attitude of Pres. McKinley toward the Filipinos. Carnegie said we civilized 8000 of them by sending them to heaven.
> I was surprised by the Chauvinistic feelings that many Americans had at the time.

Example of a personal statement to relate topic to personal life

Task 7: Review and Recite Your Notes Frequently

WHAT BRAIN RESEARCH SAYS
Periodic reviewing and reciting are the most powerful agents for building strong, clear memory traces in long term memory. Reviewing before new information is received ties the new to the older data already in memory.

After you have listened to at least four 5-10 minute TV "lectures" and have completed Tasks 1-6 for each, take out your notes of the first program you watched. This is the hard part, making sure you have begun to move data from your short term memory to your long term memory banks.

■ WEEKLY RECITE TASKS FOUR, FIVE AND SIX.

Reviewing prevents the forgetting process and reinforces long term memory. Spend about five or ten minutes on weekly reviews of each lecture.

1. Glance through your personal restatements on the left side of the right hand page. Look away.

2. Try to recite as many of the main ideas as you can based on your restatements.

3. Recite the statement of the organizational pattern of the lecture.

4. Recite your answers to questions relating to your personal experiences.

■ BEFORE THE NEXT LECTURE RECITE TASKS FOUR, FIVE, AND SIX OF THE PREVIOUS LECTURE.

Reciting before a new lecture will link the new material you are about to hear to the old information already in long term memory and make the new learning easier. While you will not be able to do this during TV training, it is a must before each regular class lecture.

1. Recite your previous notes based on your restatements.

2. Recite the statement of the organizational pattern of the previous lecture.

3. Recite your answers to questions relating to your own life of the previous lecture.

■ TEACH A "LESSON" ON THE MATERIAL OF THIS LECTURE

Teach a lesson to an imaginary class or a group of friends with whom you study. Prepare your lesson based on your Personal Restatements in Task 4.

■ USE MNEMONICS TO HELP YOU MEMORIZE YOUR ANSWERS

Use acrostics, acronyms, word-image asssociations, and songs based on the data in your answers.

Task 8: Write An Exam Question Based on the Lecture

■ **WRITE AN EXAM QUESTION IN THE "POSSIBLE EXAM QUESTION" SECTION ON THE LEFT PAGE.**

1. Think of the main ideas of the lecture. If you were the teacher, what would you want your students to be able to write about one facet of the lecture.

2. Frame one question preferably beginning with "why," "how," or "explain." Such questions require higher level thinking skills.

3. Frame other "fact" questions beginning with "list," "describe," "who," "what," "when," "state," "define," or "identify." These require students to simply recall facts.

> How did Pres. Teddy Roosevelt
> serve as a peace maker
> in the Russo - Japanese War?

Illustration of student's possible exam questions

Taking Notes in Class
Typical Student's Handwritten Left Hand Page

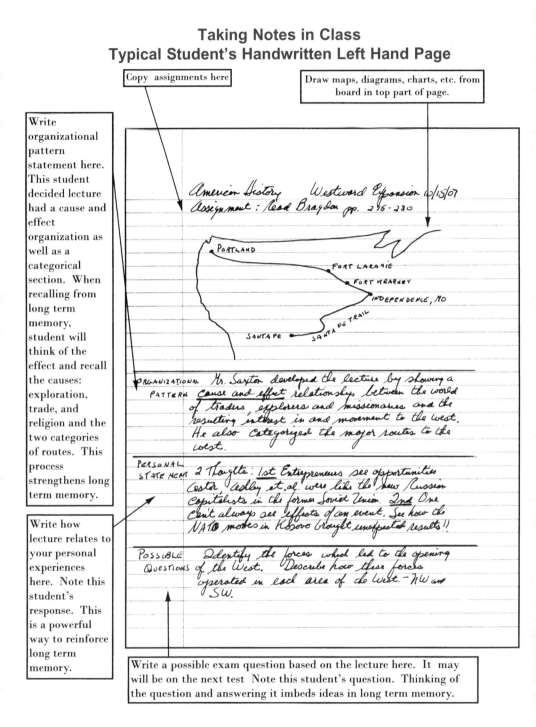

Copy assignments here

Draw maps, diagrams, charts, etc. from board in top part of page.

Write organizational pattern statement here. This student decided lecture had a cause and effect organization as well as a categorical section. When recalling from long term memory, student will think of the effect and recall the causes: exploration, trade, and religion and the two categories of routes. This process strengthens long term memory.

Write how lecture relates to your personal experiences here. Note this student's response. This is a powerful way to reinforce long term memory.

Write a possible exam question based on the lecture here. It may will be on the next test Note this student's question. Thinking of the question and answering it imbeds ideas in long term memory.

Taking Notes in Class
Typical Student's Handwritten Right Hand

This student started numbering main topics but didn't continue formal outlining. While doing Task 2, student added dashes, stars, and underlining for emphasis. Perfectly OK. Use the symbols and marks easiest for you.

Personal Restatement Column Write summaries here.

Draw vertical line two inches from left edge.

Write full lecture notes here.

Note ➜ for **to** in route description.

Student used stars to show main ideas.

Student used dashes to show supporting ideas.

Note abbreviation. **bldg.** for **building.**

Note **M** for **miles.**

Note **X** for **across,** ✔ for **down,** ➜ for **to.**

Note **Col. R.** for **Columbia River.**

Note **w/** for **with.**

Student drew symbols to represent each Personal Restatement summary.

Topic: Westward Expansion   10/15/07   ①

Explorers + Traders began movement to NW

Mexican trade began movement to SW

Missionaries brought religion loved land Motivated East friends to move West

2 Main Routes Land - Oregon Trail Sea - Cape Horn or Panama

① Explorers' + Traders' Roles
NW
* Jefferson sent Lewis + Clark 1804. Route:
Missouri R.→ Rockies → Columbia R.→ Pacific
* Fur traders flwd. J. J. Astor: Amer. Fur Co.
Wm. Ashley: Rocky Mtn Fur Co.

SW
* Trade w/ Mexican Wm. Bednell 1st.
Many flwd. Opened Santa Fe Trail
(Missouri → Santa Fe
— Used wagon caravans

② Missionaries' Role in NW
* Native Americans wanted preacher after traders.
* Methodists sent ministers 1834
* Presbyterians / Congregationalists follow.
* Rom. Catholics founded missions 1840
* Preachers taught religion + farming + bldg.
* Missionaries loved climate, soil. Told East friends who flwd.

③ Movement to Oregon
* Overland - Oregon trail 2000m Dangerous
— Indep. Mo. x Plains x Rockies ↓ Col. R.→ Pacific
— 5-6 mos. 120 people first trip
* Sea routes - Easier but longer
— ○ Cape Horn or
— X Panama Isthmus - Disease killed many

4-23

PRACTICE, PRACTICE, PRACTICE

In order to develop a skill and embed it in your procedural memory you must drill, drill, drill until all the nerves and muscles are conditioned to respond automatically.

Training with short, five to ten minute TV segments should build your confidence and develop your automatic procedural memory for note taking. Memorize your personal shorthand abbreviations so they become automatic. Continue training until you can write really rapid notes. After a couple of weeks, you should be getting most of the speaker's words down. Be alert for oral and visual cues. Be absolutely certain you are identifying main ideas, definitions and examples.

The tough components of note taking are re-phrasing main ideas into your own words and reciting from memory. When you can recite your notes without peeking you have succeeded and you are on your way to becoming an A+ student.

Actual Classroom Work

When you have mastered note taking in the practice TV sessions and are ready to use it in your actual classes, be ready to review and recite all of your lecture notes on a weekly basis. This will require diligence on your part. As the semester progresses, you will find that you have many pages of notes to review and recite. However, if you do this task regularly, you will find that the recitations become easier and easier as the data is reinforced in your long term memory and is easily recalled. You will be thrilled when you ace test after test!

Chapter 5
Taking Notes From Texts

When you read a textbook, working memory receives stimuli from the printed page. Immediately, connections are made to the long term semantic, emotional, episodic, conditioned response, and spatial memory banks. The new data tries to fit on any existing frameworks and will connect with old data in long term memory. For example, if you are reading a poem, information about the new poem will hook on to already stored ideas of rhyme, alliteration, and scansion. Emotional and episodic memories will also be stimulated by the new poem's content.

These connections will help you with your task to read, digest, and get the new information into long term memory so it can be recalled. You need to learn the new material to be sure it will be available for your use in an activity or when your knowledge will be tested on an examination.

As you know from the earlier chapters of this book, you must do everything you can to lay down powerful, clear ideas in your memory banks if you are to be successful in recalling and learning new information. In this respect, note taking from texts and note taking in class share the same goals.

However, some techniques for taking notes from texts differ from those for taking notes in class. For example, there is no need for speed writing. Within limits, you can work at your own rate and at your own time.

A track and field athlete has to develop different skills to be able to run 100 meter sprints, middle distance 800 meter races, and relays. So you will have to learn some new components of your procedural memory note taking skills to succeed in taking notes from texts.

Should You Use Your Computer To Take Notes From Texts Or Should You Handwrite?

The answer was "no" to using your computer when taking notes in class because it appears that for most users the difficulties outweigh the advantages. Foremost was the problem of keeping up with the lecturer while juggling mouse, keyboard and possibly a stylus. However, when taking notes from texts there is no speaker to follow and no rush to get notes down quickly. So the answer now is "yes."

ADVANTAGES OF COMPUTER NOTE TAKING

First, your notes will be clearer and easier to read.

Second, it is simple to add enhancements such as changing type font and size, adding underlines, bolding, and even adding color to make words stand out.

Third, you can add pictures and shapes. "Star bursts", arrows, squares, and "comic strip type balloons" can be inserted near a note. Choose Picture and Auto Shapes from the Insert menu in Microsoft Word to reach inserts. You will need to practice selecting and adding these enhancements.

Fourth, word processing, the act of turning your thoughts into words on the computer screen actually helps reinforce long term memory.

Because there are two methods, computer note takers can decide which of the two described below to use.

Instructions for preparing notebooks for handwritten note taking are on pages 5-9 to 5-11.

HOW TO PREPARE YOUR NOTEBOOK FOR COMPUTER NOTE TAKING

Method 1 - Using Text Boxes - 2 Page Layout

1. Open a new Folder in My Documents. Label it with your course title such as History 1.1. or English 2.
2. Open a new file in Microsoft Word. Use Save as to save it as Course Title Master Page Left. Choose Text Box from the Insert Menu. The mouse pointer turns into a + sign.
3. Move the pointer to create rectangular text boxes as shown on the sample on the next page. You can change the size of the boxes by clicking and grabbing one of the eight sizing handles and dragging to the size you want. Text boxes can be moved by grabbing one of the borders and dragging it to a new location on the page.
4. Place the headings in the appropriate text boxes as shown on the sample on the next page.
5. Repeat the procedure and use Save as to save the second page as Course Title Master Page Right.
6. Open each Master Page when you begin to take notes of the first chapter. Save the left page as Chapter 1 Left and the date. Save the right page as Chapter 1 Right and the date. Fill in all the boxes as you complete the Tasks in this chapter. Be sure to save the files.
7. Each time you take notes in a new chapter follow the procedure in 6 above but use Save as to change the file names to the appropriate Chapter number Left and Chapter number Right with dates. You will always have the Master Pages available.
8. Park all the files in the file folder in My Documents as explained in Number 1 above.

Check the sample pages on 5-4 and 5-5 to see how the two pages should look.

Computer Method 1 - Text Boxes - 2 Page Layout
Left Page

Date	Title	Chapter	Pages

Advanced Organizer - Outline	Questions

Chapter Summary

Charts, Graphs, Picture

Possible Test Questions

New Vocabulary

The labeled boxes on the page above are text boxes. Inserting text boxes seems complicated, but you will find they are easy to use. If you can't fit everything in a text box you can make it larger or reduce font size.

Computer Method 1 - Text Boxes - 2 Page Layout
Right Page

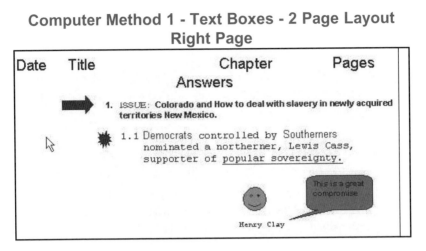

The illustration above shows some of the many enhancements available. Initially, type your notes in one font as you finish Tasks 1-4. After completing Task 4, look over your notes and decide how you want to make them stand out. Then add the special fonts, colors, and other enhancements that will be meaningful to you.

In this example, a blue arrow, a starburst, a smile face, and a comic style balloon have been added to improve this student's notes. In addition, he used color to highlight a sentence and some important words as well as underlining.

After experimenting, select just a few enhancements and standardize their use. For example, you might want to use one color and one font size and bold to set off main ideas. Starbursts, arrows and other enhancements should be reserved for other special uses, but be consistent so that when you review your notes, the enhancements will be helpful and not confusing.

TIP: Choose Tool Bars and Drawing from the View menu to add the Drawing Tool Bar to your screen to avoid having to choose Pictures from the Insert menu each time.

Method 2 - No Text Boxes - 3 Page Layout

1. Open a new Folder in My Documents. Label it with your course title such as History 1.1. or English 201.

2. Open 3 new files in Microsoft Word. Use Save as to Save them as Course Title Master Page One, Course Title Master Page 2, and Course Title Master Page 3. Insert the headings as shown on pages 5-7and 5-8.

3. Open each Master Page when you begin to take notes of the first chapter. Use Save as to save Page 1 as Chapter 1 First Page and the date. Save Page 2 as Chapter 1 Second Page and the date. Save Page 3 as Chapter 1 Third Page and the date.

4. Fill in all the boxes as you complete the Tasks in this chapter. Be sure to save the files.

5 Each time you take notes in a new chapter or on a new day follow the procedures 3 and 4 above. Use Save as to change the file names to the appropriate Chapter number and date on each of the three pages. You will always have the blank Master Pages available when you begin to take notes each day.

6. Park all the files in the file folder in My Documents as explained in Number 1 above.

Computer Method 2 - No Text Boxes - 3 Page Layout
First Page

Date	Title		Chapter	Pages

Outline

Chapter Summary

Charts, Graphs, Pictures

Possible Test Questions

New Vocabulary

Page 1

Microsoft Word does not easily allow typing in columns. If you set up a two column page, Word will finish the left column and then run the copy up to the top of the second column. You can get around this by using the Tab key to move words across the center of the page, but it is tedious to keep the answers to your questions from slipping to the left across the page to end up in your questions.

It is easier just to set up a third page as shown. Your notes will be easier to type and easier to read. You will have a lot more flexibility to type quickly rather than trying to get the Tab key to move words where you want them.

Computer Method 2 - No Text Boxes - 3 Page Layout
Second and Third Pages

Pages 2 and 3 below are shown smaller than Page 1 on the previous page in order to fit them on this page. However, all three pages will be the same size in your word processor.

Date	Titlo	Chapter	Pagcs
		Questions	

Date	Title	Chapter	Pages
		Answers	

Page 2   Page 3

As you can see, you will have much more flexibility in typing with this arrangement. Each time you take notes on an assigned reading you will open three new pages. Regardless of which method you select after each session choose Save as from the File menu and save it with new chapter, page numbers, and dates. You can keep these files in a Word file or your My Documents file in a folder with the title of the course.

You can print out your notes if you are more comfortable handling paper and enhance them with written highlighting or drawings. You can e-mail them to friends for sharing and online chats or discussions.

You might want to try all three methods; the two computer tactics and the handwritten one.

HOW TO PREPARE YOUR NOTEBOOK FOR HANDWRITTEN NOTETAKING

LEFT HAND PAGE

1. Top line: **Date   Text Title   Chapter   Pages**

2. Draw a vertical line about six and a half inches down the center of the page

3. Label top of left column: **Outline**

4. Label right column: **Questions**

5. Draw a horizontal line across the middle of the page

8. Rule three horizontal lines to divide the bottom of the page into four equal parts

9. Label Top Space: **Chapter Summary**

10. Label Second Space: **Maps, Charts, Graphs**

11. Label Third Space: **Possible Test Questions**

12. Label Fourth Space: **New Vocabulary**

RIGHT HAND AND FOLLOWING PAGES

1. Top line: **Date   Text Title   Chapter   Pages**

2. Label left margin: **Chapter Heads**

3. Label top of page: **Answers**

Handwritten Method
Sample Left Hand Page

DATE	TEXT TITLE		CHAPTER	PAGES

OUTLINE	QUESTIONS

CHAPTER SUMMARY

CHARTS - GRAPHS - MAPS - PICTURES

POSSIBLE EXAM QUESTIONS

NEW VOCABULARY

THE LEFT HAND PAGE SHOULD LIKE THE ONE ABOVE

Handwritten Method
Sample Right Hand Page

DATE   TEXT TITLE   CHAPTER   PAGES

CHAPTER   ANSWERS
HEADS

THE RIGHT HAND PAGE SHOULD LIKE THE ONE ABOVE

Task 1: Gather Materials

■ BE BUSINESS-LIKE

1. Establish a business-like environment. Be sure you have a clean, well-lighted, uncluttered study area without distractions of magazines, radio, or friends.

2. Have all materials at hand: Pencils, erasers, pens, hi-lighters, a good collegiate dictionary, notebook.

■ ESTABLISH A POSITIVE ATTITUDE

1. Approach the task positively. Sit at your desk or table on the edge of your seat. Be determined to get all you can from the text. Get rid of negative thoughts such as "This is too hard." or "How will I ever finish this assignment?"

2. Make a positive mental image of yourself working confidently through the text and succeeding. Repeat this image making twice a day for a minute or two every day you are taking notes.

3. Relate the reading to your long term personal goals. Tell yourself, "When I master this reading, I will be on my way to an A."

Task 2: First Reading
Make an Advance Organizer

WHAT BRAIN RESEARCH SAYS
Semantic memory is improved when you add new facts to an organizational framework that already exists in you memory.

An advance organizer provides the brain with a framework on which to attach new information.

■ CREATE AN ADVANCE ORGANIZER

1. Read the preface, introduction, or foreword if this is your first assignment in the text. You will find the author's motivation and intent for writing the book.

2. Read the table of contents to see how the text is organized and to get an overview. Look for chronological, cause and effect, or topical arrangements.

3. Read the summary at the beginning or end of the chapter if included. Summarize it in the space you labeled "Chapter Summary" on the left page.

4. Note locations in the chapter of graphs, charts, tables or illustrations on the left page in the space labeled,"Graphs, Charts, Maps, and Pictures."

5. Read any end of chapter questions. Jot them down under "Possible Test Questions" on the left page. Many teachers base test questions on those in the text. Think of these questions as you read because the answers will be found in the text.

■ PREPARE THE OUTLINE

1. Skim through the assignment and note chapter headings and sub-headings.

2. Make an outline on the left page in the column labeled "Outline" using the major headings and sub-headings of the chapter. Use the Harvard outline or decimal form:

Decimal Outline

1. Main topic
   - 1. 1. Sub-Topic
   - 1. 2. Sub-Topic
       - 1. 2. 1. Sub-Topic
       - 1. 2. 2. Sub-Topic

Harvard Outline

I. Main topic
   - A. Sub-topic
   - B. Sub-topic
       - 1. Sub-topic
       - 2. Sub-topic

■ REVIEW THE PRECEDING CHAPTER IF RELATED

Read your notes of the preceding chapter to tie the new information you are about to read to the data you previously learned.

■ LEARN NEW VOCABULARY

1. Skim the chapter for special technical vocabulary. It is vital that you understand the unique vocabulary of each subject. Trying to read without first mastering these terms will severely limit your ability to understand and learn the material.

2. Look for a glossary at the end of the chapter. If there is one, copy definitions on 3 x 5 inch cards. Many texts print special words in bold and/or italics the first time they are used. Memorize the definitions.

3. Find new vocabulary words by skimming the chapter. Copy each new vocabulary word on a 3 x 5 inch card and look up its meaning in a good, collegiate dictionary. Write the definition, etymology (the origin of the word) antonym and a piece of the sentence in which you found the word so you will learn it in the context in which it was used.

4. Find new vocabulary words in your daily reading of newspapers and magazines. Add any other new words to your pack of cards. Carry the cards with you and recite the meanings whenever you get a minute. The richer your vocabulary, the more your comprehension and reading speed will improve.

5. Write the new vocabulary words in the section labeled "New Vocabulary" on the left hand page.

Task 3: First Reading
Formulate Questions

WHAT BRAIN RESEARCH SAYS
When a criterion task, or what you need to learn, is clear you learn more easily. By preparing questions you set the criterion task and you focus clearly on what you have to learn.

■ DECIDE HOW MUCH TIME TO SPEND ON THE ASSIGNMENT

1. Set a time limit. Don't drag on endlessly. Set a good pace and keep at it.

2. Read easy material at the rate of fifteen pages per hour. Difficult stuff might take five to seven pages per hour.

■ FORMULATE QUESTIONS AND WRITE THEM ON THE ADVANCE ORGANIZER - OUTLINE PAGE

1. Re-phrase as questions the headings you wrote in the "Outline" column and jot them down in the "Questions" column on the right side of the left page. For example, a topic, "Causes of Poverty," would become "What are the causes of poverty?" You will establish a "criterion task" so you will know what you have to learn. You will also identify the main ideas.

2. Try to locate the answers to your questions by quickly reading all the pages of the assignment. You will get some preliminary ideas of the answers.

Task 4: Second Reading
Read Powerfully

> ### WHAT BRAIN RESEARCH SAYS
> You will remember more if you are motivated to learn, if you link new facts to the advance organizer, and if you make the learning meaningful. It is easier to learn if you break material into small chunks.

■ STAY FOCUSED AND MOTIVATED

1. Prepare psychologically. Understand that textbook reading is difficult. Psych yourself as if you were about to climb a mountain or attack some other physical task. Make a mental image of yourself succeeding. Don't even think about reading in bed!

2. Get motivated. Don't approach the reading in anger toward your instructor because you think he or she was mean to assign this difficult material. Think about the value you will get from the reading, about how it will help raise your grade, and about how it will affect your career. You are doing this for you. Stop for a minute and again make a mental image of yourself succeeding with this assignment.

■ BREAK THE READING INTO SMALLER CHUNKS

1. Plan to read "chunks" over several hours spread out during one day. Don't try to read difficult material in a single, long session.

2. Read for 30 minutes and take 5. Get up and walk about. Have a cup of coffee or a glass of milk.

■ READ ACTIVELY

1. Read very difficult material out loud.

2. Do not highlight during the second reading. Before you know it, you will be highlighting too much. You will not truly understand what is important until you finish the second reading.

3. Make check marks or notes in the margin if you own the book. These can be erased, left or added to later when you have a better idea of what is important.

4. Write definitions of difficult vocabulary and questions you want to ask your teacher as well as your own ideas and comments in the margin, but only if you own the book.

5. Recite aloud in your own words what you have read at the end of each paragraph.

6. Read critically. Is the author stating facts or opinions? Is the author biased? Do you agree with the author's conclusions? How does this author's ideas fit with the ideas of others? How does the text relate to the lecture notes you took in class?

7. Problem understanding? Put a big question mark in the margin and make a note to ask your teacher to explain in class. Continue reading. The following material may help you understand the passage that troubled you.

8. Relate the information to your personal life. Ask whether you are reminded of an emotional event in your life. Do the ideas affect me emotionally? Do I agree or disagree strongly? Do these ideas upset me? Make me angry, sad, or happy?

■ FIND THE ANSWERS TO YOUR QUESTIONS

1. Read strategically. As you read each paragraph or page, be sure you are reading to get the answer to one of your listed questions. As you find the answer, summarize it in your own words.

2. Write the summary answers to your "Questions" in the Advance Organizer page. Write the number of the question and the answer in the "Answer" column on the right hand page of your notebook.

3. Insert diagrams, maps, symbols and timelines as appropriate anywhere on the Answer page to reinforce semantic memory.

■ STRIVE TO INCREASE READING SPEED

1. Read rapidly, but not a a speed that interferes with comprehension. Move a 5 x 8 inch card down the page above the line you are reading to prevent eye regressions or looking back at words you have already read.

2. Reduce the number of eye fixations on each line. Try not to read one word at a time, but rather strive to "take in" whole phrases or groups of words in each fixation.

3. Don't attempt to match the ridiculous "speed reading" claims of being able to read a whole page in one glance suggested by some "speed reading" gurus. In general, comprehension improves with increases in speed and speed increases with improvement in comprehension. Good average speed is 250 words per minute.

Task 5: Third Reading
Recite

■ RECITE

1. Look at the first question on the Advance Organizer page. Quickly, read the first section of the text again. Check the answer to the first question you wrote in your notebook during the second reading. Is it accurate? If not, revise it.

2. Recite the answer to the first question out loud without looking at your notes. Check to see if you recited correctly. Recite the answers to all your questions, proceeding section by section.

4. Recite as much of the chapter summary in the text and/or the one you wrote in Task 2. Check for accuracy.

5. Stress the recall of major concepts rather than details.

6. Do one more quick reading with your highlighter. Now that you know which parts of the text are truly important, highlight in your notes only those. The highlighted words and phrases will help you during reviews.

7. Use mnemonics: acronyms, acrostics, word-image asssociations and songs to bolster your memory.

Task 6: Review

WHAT BRAIN RESEARCH SAYS
Periodic reviews reinforce semantic and other long term memory banks by carving deep, clear memory traces. Each review strengthens the memory.

■ REVIEW FREQUENTLY

1. Recite the answers to your questions the day after your third reading. You may have forgotten some information, but it will quickly come back.

2. Each week spend five minutes to review your notes. Recite the main ideas and answers to questions.

3. Before tests, review your notes. Recite the main ideas, and answers to your questions for all the units that will be tested. You should ace the test!

■ WRITE A TEST QUESTION

1. Use "how," "why, and "explain" to open questions that will elicit in-depth responses.

2. Use 'who," "what", "when," "list," "define," and "describe" to elicit factual information. Write the answers to your questions.

■ TEACH A LESSON

Teach a lesson to an imaginary class or a group of friends with whom you study. Use the answers to your questions as a basis for the lesson.

Taking Notes From Texts
Typical Student's Handwritten Left Hand Page

Task 2. Begin developing an advance organizer by quickly copying major heads and sub-heads of the chapter using Harvard outline style in the left hand column.

Task 3. Rephrase the headings as questions in the right hand column.

Task 2. Continue development of the advance organizer by summarizing printed chapter summary.

Task 2. Describe illustrations, charts, diagrams, etc. This sample describes a brochure, *Emigrants Guide to California* which appears in this text.

Task 3. Write additional questions based on an overview printed at the beginning of the chapter.

Task 2. Write new, special vocabulary words This student found *popular sovereignty*.

10/15/07 History of a Free Nation Ch 14 Sec 1 pp. 386-390

OUTLINE	QUESTIONS
1. Election of 1848	1. What was the major issue of the election of 1848?
1.1 Democrats + Whigs	1.1 What were the positions of the Democrats + Whigs?
1.2. Free Soil Party	1.2 What was the Free Soil Party?
2 California Question	2. What was the California Question?
2.1 Application for Statehood	2.1 What happened when California applied for statehood?
2.2. Compromise of 1850	2.2 What was the Compromise of 1850?

Chapter Summary - Deep political + social issues divided the country. South thought slavery a "positive good". Northerners + Westerners opposed. Compromise was failing. Acquisition of New Mexico and Cal. forced the issue.

Charts-Graphs-Pictures - P.390 Brochure. "Emigrants Guide to California" describes routes, etc. Part of Gold Rush life. 3 Routes - 1. Across Panama 2. Around Cape Horn 3. Overland.

Possible Test Questions: 1. Evaluate the impact of slavery on the 1848 presidential election. 2. Explain why the admission of California created hot debates on slavery. 3. List 4 provisions of the Compromise of 1850.

New Vocabulary - Popular Sovereignty - Voters decide slavery question in each territory.

The headings, sub-headings, description of the illustration, and other information on these pages were drawn from:

Bragdon, Henry W., Samuel P. McCutchen, and Donald A. Ritchie. *History of a Free Nation*. New York: Glencoe/McGraw-Hill, 1998. Chapter 14, Section 1.

Taking Notes From Texts
Typical A Student's Handwritten Right Hand Page

Read difficult passages aloud.

Stop at the end of each paragraph and explain aloud what you read.

Write answers to each question after reciting aloud.

Try to increase speed and comprehension.

Task 4. Read powerfully to find the answers to the questions based on the headings and sub-headings. Write answers on the right hand and following pages.

10/15/07 *History of a Free Nation Ch.14 Se.1 pp. 386-390*
ANSWERS

Election of ① Issue- How to deal with slavery in newly
1848   acquired territories of Colorado and New Mexico.
       1.1 Democrats, controlled by Southerners nominated
Democrats, a northerner, Lewis Cass, supporter of popular sovereignty.
Whigs   Whigs, mostly Northerners, nominated Zachary
       Taylor, Southern slave holder!! Whigs avoided
       slavery question - stressed Taylor's military deeds.
Free   1.2 Free Soilers - Emerged as 3rd Party from anti-
Soilers   slavery North Democrats + "Conscience Whigs" - Motto:
       "Free Soil, Free Speech, Free Labor, Free Men" Nominated
       Van Buren. Deprived Cass of NY's 36 Electoral Votes!!

California ② After gold discovered 1848, population grew by 95,000
Question   and the slavery question arose.
       2.1 Statehood - Military could not stop crime, violence.
Application Taylor called convention 1849 to set up gov't + forbid
       slavery. Applied as free state giving free states majority.
       South threatened to secede.
       2.2 Compromise - Henry Clay arranged.
Compromise   North - 1. Cal. admitted as Free State
of 1850   2. Slave trade, not slavery forbidden in
                    D.C.
       South 1. Stronger fugitive slave law passed
             2. Mexican Cession - Divided Utah +
                New Mexico into 2 territories with slavery
                question decided by popular sovereignty.
       Compromise proved to be only
       a temporary truce.

Task 5. Read first section of text again and check written answer for accuracy. Look away from notes and recite answer to first question.

Task 5. Read printed chapter summary again and recite your written summary on left page.

Task 5. One last reading to highlight important words.

Task 6. The day after the third reading in Task 5 recite the answers to the questions on the left page without looking at your notes. Spend just 10 minutes reciting. Once weekly spend 5 minutes reciting the answers. Before tests, recite the answers again.

Taking Notes From Texts
Typical Student's Computer Left Hand Page

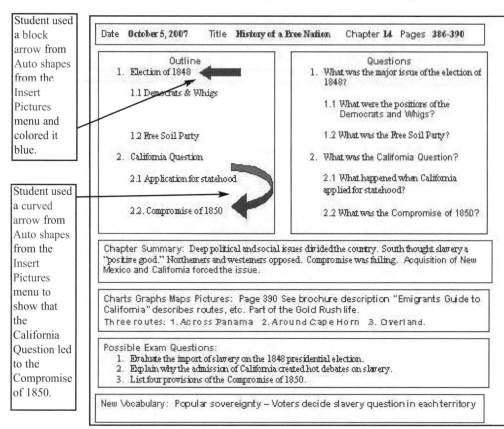

This student used color to highlight important phrases. Although this illustration is restricted to the color blue, you may select from a palette of colors. For example, you might want to highlight the main headings in blue and the sub-heads in red.

Note that two different fonts and two font sizes were used as well as the Bold from the Toolbar. Computer note taking allows you to embellish your notes to make them as powerful as you like.

Taking Notes From Texts
Typical Student's Computer Right Hand Page

Chapter Heads	Answers
Election of 1848	1. Issue: How to deal with slavery in newly acquired territories of Colorado and New Mexico.
Democrats	1.1 Democrats, controlled by Southerners, nominated, Lewis Cass, a supporter of popular sovereignty.
Whigs	Whigs, mostly Northerners, nominated Zachary Taylor, a Southern slave holder!!. Whigs avoided the slavery question – stressed Taylor's military deeds.
Free Soilers	1.2 Free Soilers – Emerged as 3rd Party from anti-slavery northern Democrats and "Conscience Whigs." Their motto: "Free Soil, Free Speech, Free Labor, Free Man." They nominated Van Buren and deprived Cass of NY State's 36 Electoral Votes.
California Question	2. Issue: After gold discovered in 1848, population grew by 95,000 and the slavery question arose.
Application for Statehood	2.1 Statehood – Military could not stop crime and violence. Taylor called convention in 1847 to set up a government and to forbid slavery. California applied as a free state giving the free states a majority. The South threatened to secede.
Compromise of 1850	2.2 Compromise – Henry Clay arranged the Compromise of 1850.
	North – 1. California admitted as a Free State. 2. Slave trade, but not slavery forbidden in D.C.
	South – 1. Stronger fugitive slave law passed. 2. Mexican Cession – Divided Utah and New Mexico into two territories with slavery question decided by Popular Sovereignty. Compromise proved to be only a temporary truce.

On this page the student used fine arrows from the Drawing Toolbar. You can get it by clicking on View Toolbars Drawing

On this page the student used several of the same techniqes, but he also added a starburst colored blue to show the importance of the growing slavery question. This is obtained from either the Drawing Toolbar or the Insert Picture AutoShape Toolbar.

Notice that under the Compromise of 1850 in the Chapter Heads column, he inserted a picture of a person holding two fighters apart. Many pictures can be added from the Drawing Toolbar or the Insert Picture Toolbar. However, be consistent and do not overdo your enhancements.

Summary

If you have been motivated to become an A+ student and if you have made note taking an automatic skill by applying the techniques outlined in this book you, no doubt, have seen your grades improve. No doubt, too, your teachers have noted your class and test performance.

The skills you have learned will be helpful in many of your future school, professional, or business activities. The ability to "keep up" with discussions in different venues, to take clear notes, and, above all, to get the data into your long term memory for future recall will bear great dividends.

Being able to read texts, professional or business reports, and journal articles rapidly and with understanding is another skill you have learned. As you go through life, you will be amazed at the amount of material in print or on the Web that you are required to read and absorb. Your newly learned automated, conditioned response to reading and digesting and remembering written material is a powerful tool that will give you many advantages.

Good luck with your new skills in school and life!

Bibliography

Goleman, D. *Emotional Intelligence.* New York: Bantam, 1995.

Jensen, E. *Teaching With the Brain In Mind.* Alexandria, VA: Association for Supervision and Curriculum Development, 1998.

Kensinger, E. A. and S. Corwin. "Memory Enhancement for Emotional Words." *Memory and Cognition* 31 (2003): 1169-1180.

Miller, George A. "The Magical Number Seven, Plus or Minus Two: Some Limits on Our Capacity for Processing Information." *The Psychology Review* 63 (1956): 81-97.

Sousa, D. *How Your Brain Learns.* Reston, VA: NAASP, 1995.

Sprenger, M. *Learning and Memory.* Alexandria, VA: Association for Supervision and Curriculum Development, 1999.

Tulving, E. "Episodic Memory From Mind To Brain." *Annual Review of Psychology* 53 (2002): 1-25.

Notes: